Indigo Angel: Poems & Prayers by

Kali Tenee'

©2018-2020 Kali Tenee'
~All rights reserved~
No part of this book may be reproduced, stored in a retrieval system, or transmitted by any means without the written permission of the author.
Editing/Book Cover Art: Kali Tenee'

THE POETRY:

light
angel's promise
my God, your/e god
holes in the whole
keep 'em safe
regrets
the weeping
t.i.m.e. (time infinity moments eternal)
better
11:11
naked in the light
#confessionsofanarcoleptic
heaven and earth
beyond
knowing
we angels
marry nostalgia
used to love me
opportunities
cure
melanin prayers
pillar
before you were thought of
who haunts you
wanderlust
so[ul] to speak: prayers
444
policing
pray away
so, who?
for the best
fear
astral angels
true love
ancestral memory
letting go
grace us
shame
domestic violets
suspension
oddly enough
blindsided
addict
smudges
we
the long and short of it
within and without
tilling
God thought
back up drive

Indigo Angel: Poems and Prayers

Prayer. Our understanding of prayer is that it is a personal plea or conversation with our Higher Power. Whosoever we believe in (if at all)...most of us believe in the authority of speaking power into things, asking "the universe" for favor, and the connectivity that comes with collective praying.

Poems. Poems are the children of poetry, (some poems are music and visual) and thereby, the art of eloquently expressing one's self within a structure of rhythm, pauses and emphasis.

Angels....I believe in angels and their presence in our lives as guardians, muses, and inspirations...and I believe it is very possible for poems and prayers to be together, a language that speaks to the soul. The God in us all. The language of angels, maybe?

Do you ever wonder about how angels come into our lives? Do you ever wonder if you've met, sat beside or loved an angel? A *real* deal angel? I marvel at the idea.

Can you imagine an angel's daily life here on Earth? What if we were their "assignments"?

They'd come to us in the form of family, friends and lovers...leaving once they've helped us find our way.

...just imagine, your life being touched by angels. Imagine them being the person you least expected to be one. How would your life change to know you were keeping company with angels, quite possibly loved by a few?

They are the beacons of love, light, inspiration and understanding. They induce change, enlightenment, life and love.

They're here to promote that change within the agency of love...LOVE. May my gift of writing be a light unto you.

~light~

we can be a light
or be light in demeanor
we can see by the light
we can be light sensitive
we can find light in love and life
we can find the shore
by the light of a beacon,
or the moon...
we can light the way
with the truth,
because truth *is* the light...
we can be light as rays
and be lit for days
we can be so light as to fade
or be the kind of light
that blinds so we can't find our way...
are you a night light?
a star's light,
a flash of light...?

...yet, even light
must give way
to the shadows...
they bring the light forward
they make light brighter
shadows bring balance
so don't forget your shadow,
without it,
you'd blow a fuse and be
completely in the dark

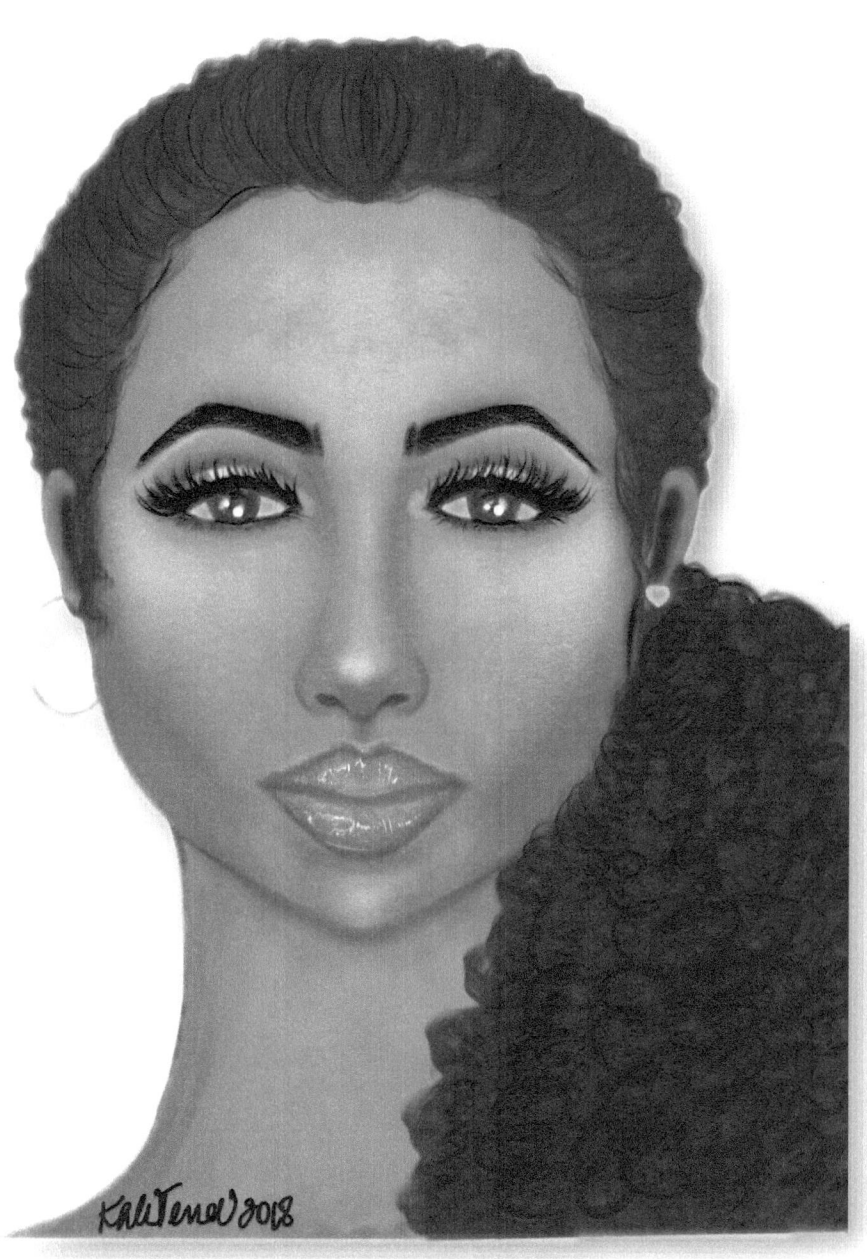

~angel's promise~

I live between
the minutes and blinks
my presence is
something like a thought
I'm there when your mind wanders
when your heart skips a beat
right in the mix of
rain turning to rays
right in the mix of
hours turning to days
somewhere deeply ensconced
in when thank you's
morph into prayers...
I'm sitting on perches
on limbs of bare trees
lifting you from low spaces
warning you from catastrophes
I've covered you
in high winds
pointed out people you should meet
I've plucked feathers from my wings
to tickle your fancy
i never sleep
eat or grow weary
i live between
the doors you open and close
I'm in the ideas clustered
a plane above...
I exist as escort in your dreams
I am an angel,
I am one of a legion...
I am in the in betweens
I am here
I promise.

everyone wants to be right about WHO it is that is responsible for souls and the faith they live by. though not all of us believe in an entity unseen to us, but imagined to be beyond the galaxies still undiscovered...we all in some way clamor for understanding about if there is indeed, someone to be revered.

~my God, your/e god~

the religion
we should rely on
shouldn't be the difference
in our tenets...
but the oneness
in our creation
what if,
we spent so much time
battling over
whose god is God
that we neglect the voice
of God *within*
Him trying to
sew the human condition together
like darning a sock
and we're too occupied
with using our
underdeveloped understanding
to toss one another about,
and miss seeing the stars
in each other's eyes
or to see the tears in God's?
...and even if
you don't believe in God
there is the image of self
in man to respect...
couldn't we just
rely on *that*?

my, my, my...we are a forgetful bunch. us humans...skin wearers, pursuers of dominion over one another. we claim we will be in the moment when we lose someone, but then we go right back into the space of oblivion. what is the value in that?

~holes in the whole~

some don't know
the value of life
until death
the void of a loved one
like the feeling of hunger
reminds us
of the nourishment
we need from tangible love
we aren't oblivious
to potential loss...
it's that,
when we're whole
we don't pain
when the oneness
is intact
we have no need
to mourn
only when the fabric
has been ripped
and we feel the draft
of a hole,
do we sense the loss of wholeness
maybe,
death is a tearing
a schism that demands
we stitch the space in time
...no matter,
we're never quite the same
once another piece goes missing.
this is the truth of death
and the fabric of life

{the climate of racial hostility and violence continues to escalate. It stands to reason, we all are praying for our loved ones as much as possible}

~keep'em safe~

out the door they go
to work,
to school,
to the corner store
and I pray...
that today,
hatred oversleeps
or takes the long road home
so that it will miss
my brother
on his way to work
my father
in a park
my sister
driving to see a friend...
I pray, that today
my loves make it home
in time for homework
dinner
date night,
...in time for *life*
please on today,
let hatred die hungry
and let my loves live long
let hatred go blind
long enough
for my son to walk by
maim hatred
make it lame
and unable...
let its memory lapse
just...
dear God,
keep'em safe

…meanwhile, we're losing time…*wasting* time, ignoring the opportunities to be with the ones who do in fact, not only make it home…but, *become* home to us.

~regrets~

on a night
thick with weary
he remembered when
his life had life

and when he
thumbed through
the scenes in his heart
the one face repeated…

her smile, laugh, touch
played like wind chimes…
he could taste the meals
and feel the feels
and it felt real…

even decades away
even seconds away…
from saying…

never mind
he's just remembering
when life had life

…when life had *her*.

dedicated to my cousin Tyshi, inspired by "punkin" and Pops

~the weeping~

the sudden change
of space in the room
when someone
opens the portal
of light to darkness,
walks out and away
to planes unknown
and leaves us weeping

preparing doesn't prepare you
for the dust
left in hand
for us, left on land
as love sails away
and...

leaves us weeping

we search our dreams
for visits
our days for signs
nature for messages...
a bird saunters near,
a bee kisses the ear,
the clouds form eyes,
the waters rise high...

leaving us weeping

the dying of kin
a friend
or lover's end
lends no words
to bear the pain
of when the skies open
and it rains mourning

...leaving us weeping.

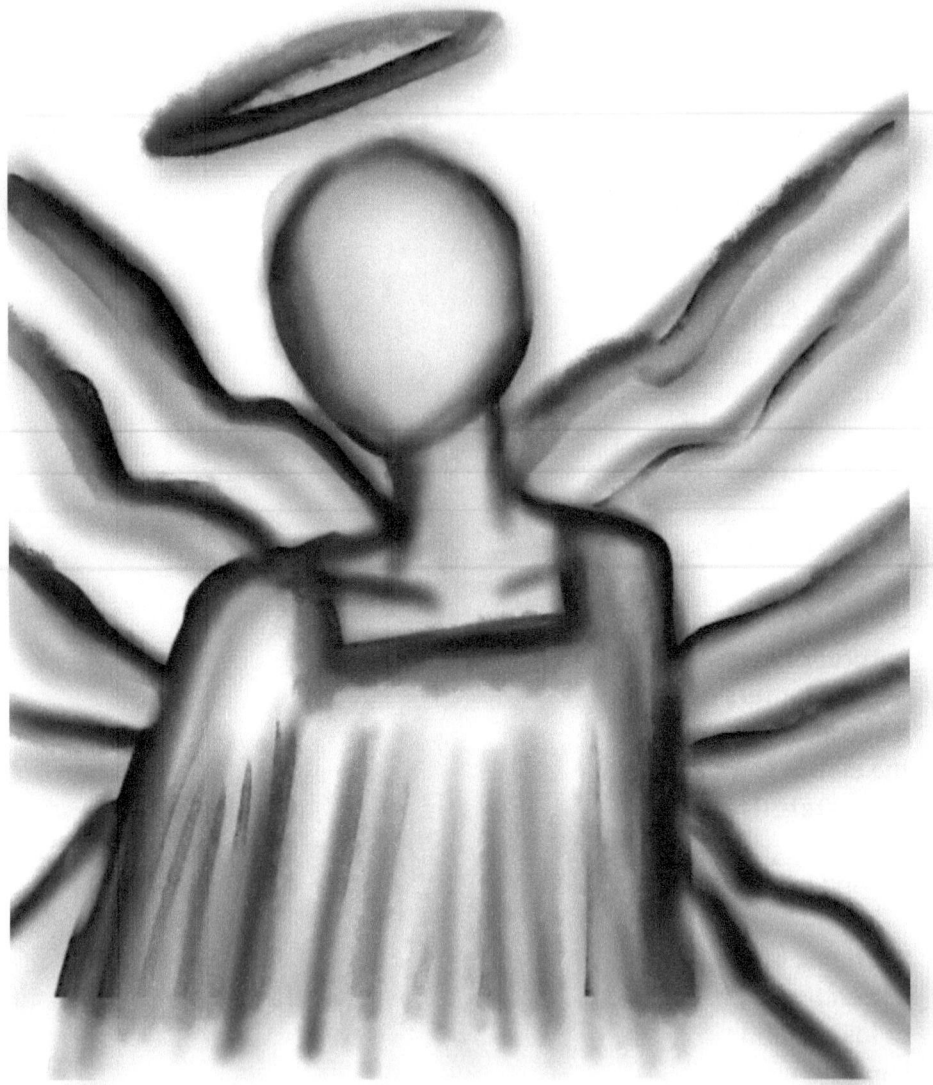

~t.i.m.e. (time infinity moments eternal) ~

time is relevant
to us,
we are old...days are long
time never seems to end
middle age is 50
and the middle ages...centuries ago
for us,
the brisk passing of a flower's bloom
or the transient lifespan of a butterfly
in comparison to our decades of life
is a flashing light
yet in the eye of the universe
with its immeasurable stars
ancient and infinite
hand in hand
with God's omniscience...
we too are perennials and monarch butterflies
a passing fancy
to the ticking of
the eternal clock
time is time is time...time and again
it is to us, what we know of us
it is to everything else
what everything is to eternity
are we even relevant?
time will tell

~better~

things should get better
we want to progress
yet we have to protest
just to key the ignition
to the land of tomorrow...
we're in twenty twenty
which feels more like
flashbacks to Juneteenth
feels like new day lynching
...bodies swinging from jail cells
and water hoses
something like
the deluding of violated rights
flooding the streets
with fear of safety

slaves slaved,
slaves were freed, but
free STILL ain't free
we seem to be circling back
360 degrees of cycling chains...
but where we going?
things should get better,
...better?
shit, most ain't met'er.

(I wrote this in 2018 but changed the year to reflect where we are now)

~11:11~

thank you, God
universe and stars
bless the maker
bless the made
aide in our ascension
keep us...guide us.
may I be found dwelling
in the greatest good intended for me
let my intentions go forth
like energy and light
in bolts of love and truth
may I master me
and honor You,
thank you.

there should never be a time, when you look at yourself and recoil with the shame the world has thrust at you. you're not the social construct of destructive conduct. you are not the regret in hindsight, you are the hope of a new day. throw away those who threw away opportunities to connect with your light. pack away the tattered fabric of hand-me-down complexes, given to you with disdain...shit that wasn't even folded and delivered with love. shit that was tossed onto you as if you were naked and ugly to the beholding eye. "put something on" is what they said with their unspoken suggestion. well, 'no thank you' is how you respond...or 'fuck you', whichever feels most authentic.

you...are not regret. you are regaling pomp and circumstance, delivered in fanfare to the world. high step into your self love...march like you're the only one twirling a baton. shame on *them* for not seeing your dope~itude. shame on *you* for giving a damn. fix that.

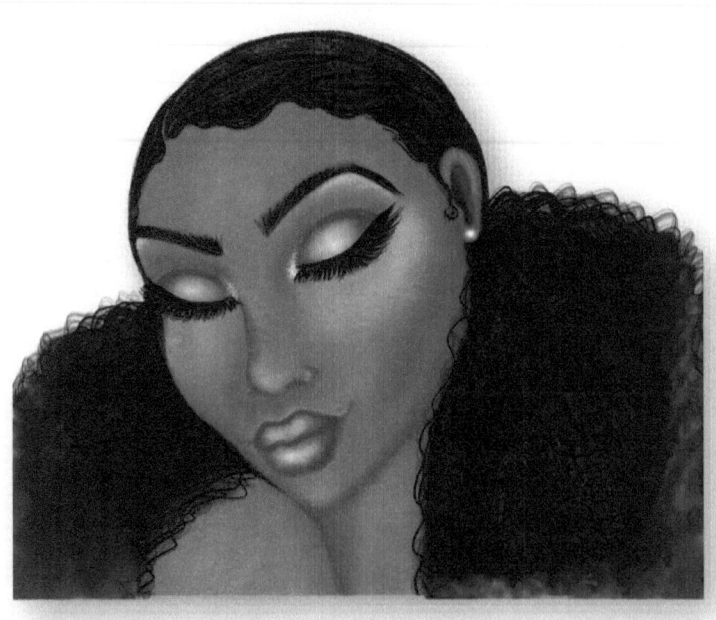

~naked in the light~

I was fat to some,
too much to hold
to own up to
to love...
to be proud of.
my rolls
were layers of reasons
why no one
should roll with me
...and I believed it
I received it
I cleaved to it
I let it become
a cloak
a covering
a comfort
I am discovering...
I withdrew from
the draw of love,
made myself
at home alone
and caved to the idea
that I was
better off untouched
the truth is
that I'm a lover
who deserves love,
my rolls deserve touch
I, and you too...
deserve to reject
the shame
of hateful fear
to be naked in the light

#confessionsofanarcoleptic

when I first
began to nod
at school...then the job
I felt ashamed
that two of my eyes
couldn't stay as wide
as the third
brightly lit,
but flickering...
I hated the disorder
threatening chaos in my life
I asked God to remove it
until,
it seemed
that my dreams
were conduits
to intuit...
my curse became my gift
as my impressions became swift
the thing that made me
feel worthless
gave birth to kisses
of astral light
connecting me to
the here and gone
to shine my light on
...alas, I found the beauty in sleep

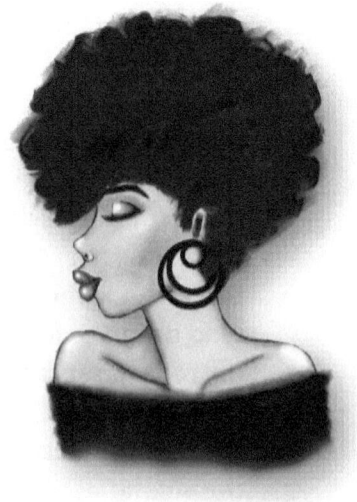

~heaven and earth~

angels,
are birthed from
the womb of the universe
souls impregnating
the universal womb...
angels,
are the transcended from the earth's deceased
the newborn
angels,
are the birthed
from the universally conceived angels
to save the souls
lost to the world
from alienation,
neglect,
and loneliness...
and gives them
"earthly wings"
to assist in guiding human hearts

heavenly wings are for the heaven born...
angels born into their purpose
for God's glory and will
earthly wings are for angels created
by other angels
come to our plane...
the ethereal wings
are visible to true "seers" and the ilk,
empaths,
Indigos
Crystal
Rainbow
and star seeds.
the earthly wings
are like antennas
receptors,
between the heavenly
and the flesh bound
they can be anyone...anywhere
it could be you...

~beyond~

[d]ashes to [d]ashes
[star]dust to [star]dust
with the speed of light
carry this message
through black holes
and nebulae

by the sound of
my voice
and the light in
my eyes...
carry this note
to the ears
of my love

through births
and rebirths
deaths
and transcending
past planes
and realms
orbits and revolutions...

I will always
meet you
in the spaces
where bodies
fall away
souls dance with comets
and desires are untethered

I love you

~knowing~

when we met
we knew...

until the
consciousness
of the world
covered our 3rd eye
with shame
awareness of eyes watching
small minded constructs
restricting wills and wants
yet unable
to glean
the ancient
ageless
connection we shared...

we knew,
and still,
we melted
into conformity
of a normalcy
we could never be

we went blind
and never again
would we see...
what we once knew
when we met...
it was always
you and me

it will always,
be you and me

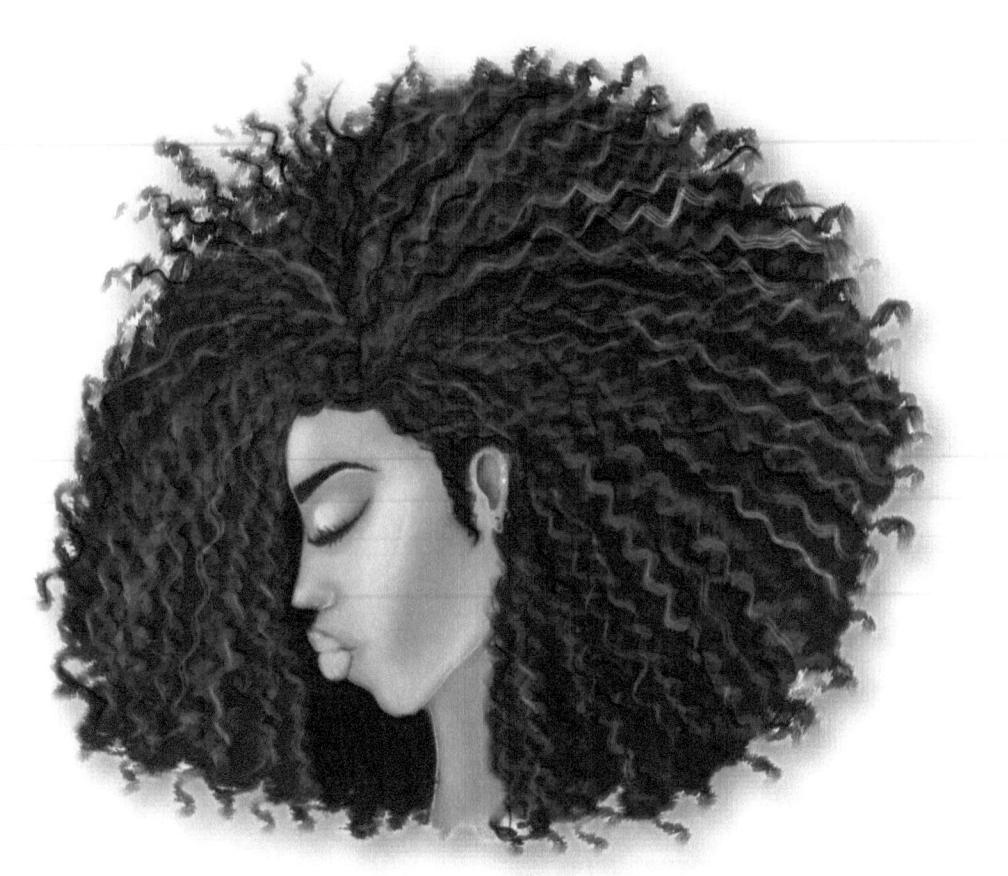

~we angels~

we angels
were born of two ways
straight from the Creator's touch
or reborn from
lost souls
by the touch of
firstborn angels...
I am Indigo born
star child blessed
angel created by angel

I heal
I feel
I touch the untouched,
even though
there are times,
when I, too...
long for tangible care
for concerned heart

...yet, my mission
at times
is to extract the pain
a needle to the ill
and drop it into
the hands of God
to become dust
and debris

we angels
were born to be brave
where hearts cower
in shadowed nooks
lepers to love
strangers to
outstretched arms

I hear/heal you...

I believe people who fall deeply in love and have a hard time moving on aren't so in love that they're unable to love again. I believe they're trapped in a memory ("drifting on a memory...ain't no place I'd rather be, than with you..."). they're coasting on a feeling they relive, with no context. Is the person the same? do they remember us like I do? Sometimes memories are beautiful and other times...they're a distorted, grotesque prison we succumb to...in the cage, with the door open.

~marry nostalgia~

you're not in love
with me
maybe it's memories
you don't even know me
i'm not the girl that I was...
maybe your life hurts
and you're looking for elixirs
and our time was nice,
but is it what's right?
you're not in love
with me...
it's a romantic fantasy
maybe it's her...
maybe it's the girl
who has stolen my identity,
pretending to be me
when all she'll ever be
is moments in time,
maybe she's who you love...
marry nostalgia

~used to love me~

many men
have loved me "when"
then...
intentions left
to the wind
fond of my face
sweet on my space
silent though,
allowing time to waste
with all the love,
the kween
of their dreams...
and still,
I am husband-less
childless
joyless...

woe to have been loved
and never have been loved

love me,
prospectively
not retrospectively
I am here now,
for I may be busy later.

~opportunities~

there are blessings
which are time stamped
moments
in a slit, carved
in space and time...
whilst others,
branded with our names
are forever ours

nothing shaped
to fit your hands
sent by the mind
of the universe...
will go undelivered.

it was always yours
and so it shall remain...
and remember,
no one can touch
what they can't reach
yours was made
for your [spiritual] height,
so everything for you
is gonna be alright

~cure~

in efforts to
come home
you promised
to fix the pain
to heal me
and wash away
the tainted memories
my love
scabbed
from scrapes
of mistakes you made
in an attempt
to escape
the state of us...

you promised
to dip me
steep me
in waters
with healing properties
and properly show me
the display
from effects
caused by affections
you staved
with the weight of your excuses...

cure me or leave me
to lie in pieces
until I piece myself together again

~melanin prayers~

you beautiful wonders
with your
ruddy reds
peeking past
darkened browns
...with your
bluest blues,
playing up
to the blackest blacks
those
yellowed hints
kissing on bronzed tans
olives with hazels
toffees with coffees

I pray your colors...
crimsons
ochres
lavenders
onyx
reds...

pop with the melanin
of a millennium of generations
shades infinity

amen

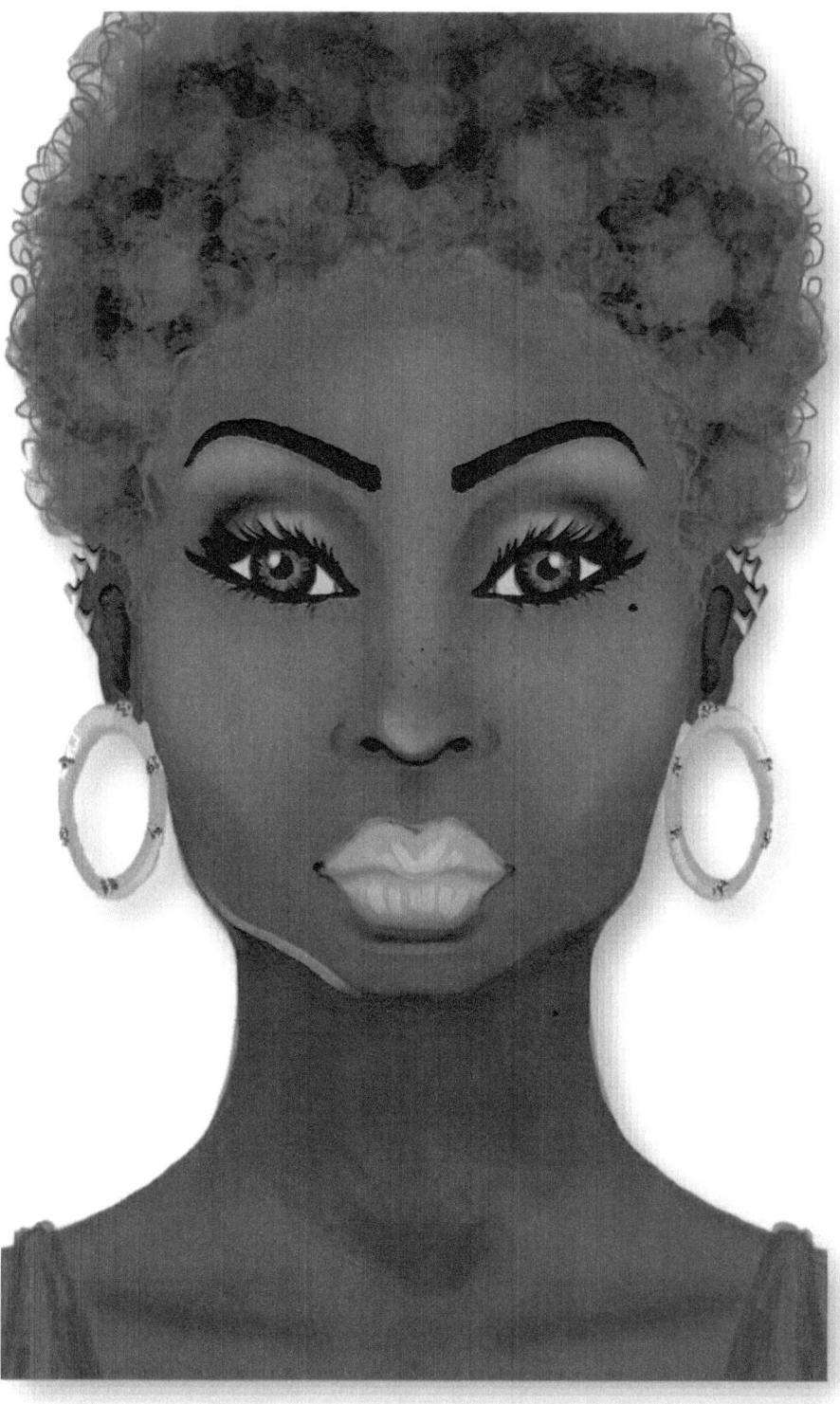

~pillar~

strength ain't strong…
at times,
strength is denial
"ain't nothing wrong"

it's a lie we offer…
"I'm good"
when the roof is collapsing
in their laps

…strength ain't strong
til you can say you're not

~before you were thought of~

we
were always here
a part of *the*
collective mind
we were [*always*]
thought
love,
and spirit
intentionally
moving...
amid other
sparks of consciousness

we were conceived
in the twilight
birthed in the dawning
of dust and water
before bodies
were frames
no given names
...just electric pulses
waiting to move
through time
to be here

we were created on purpose
that's as thoughtful as it comes

~who haunts you? ~

who is it?
whose face do you see?
the voice that stirs you...
the touch you feel...
whose laugh do you hear?
whose body
hovers over yours...
in dreams magnificent
fantasies exquisite
thoughts reminiscent
in your astral album
whose image...
slides across
in memoirs
immortalized
in flashes of light
triggered by
chills up spines
smiles conjured by promises
love captured in sighs
whose heart beats
when yours does?
pulsing in loud silence
breaking with distance
leaping...
at first
and every sight
who haunts you?
clinking chains
binding you
revisiting your spirit
waking you
shaking you
making you feel
when you're trying to forget
showing themselves
in everything you see
every moment you breathe
every reflection you see
who haunts you?
because *you* haunt ME...

~wanderlust~

shuffling on damp leaves
music in the air
the scent of rained rain
fog like condensed cool
trees afire
with autumn shades
as I capture nature...
slideshows of us play
vividly still
live video of your voice echoes...
soulful sounds
rhythm, no blues
just the residue of
a place I'll never go again
I lust to wander...to be where you are

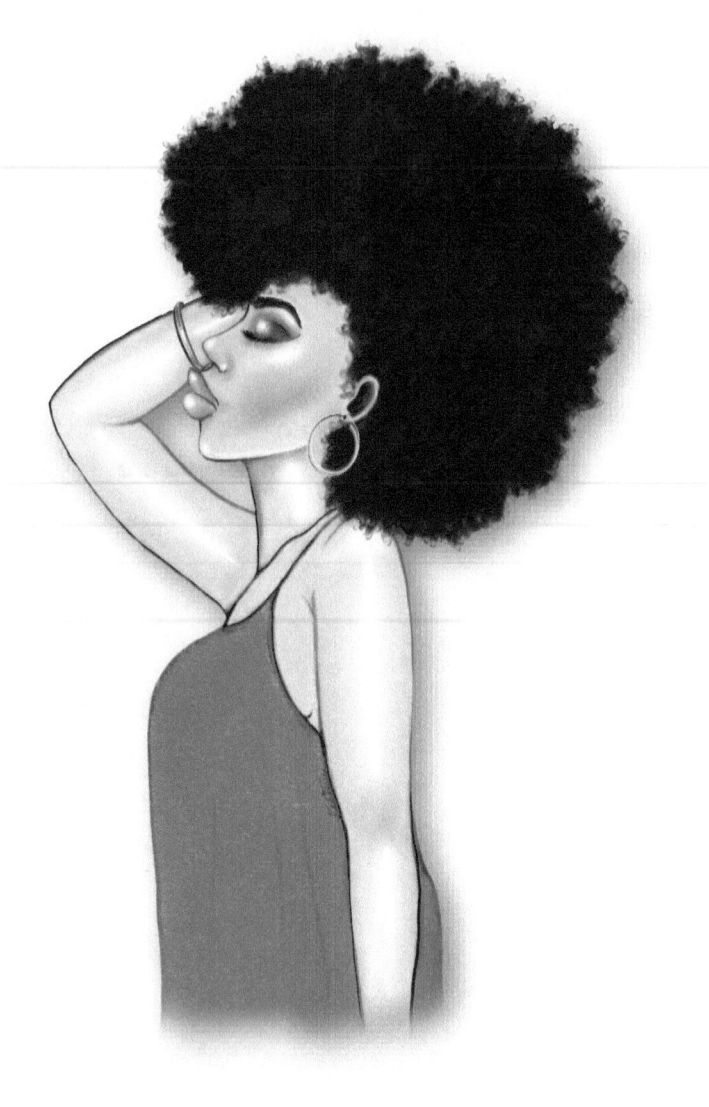

We pray. We ask. We beckon and besiege. We talk to, plead to, and venerate...through prayer. There are so many ways we speak to the supreme, universe...God. How does your soul speak?

~so[ul] to speak: prayers~

it's a kind of prayer
I guess...
when our ponderings
meet midair,
our guides
conspiring to speak
in the dark
nudging us to meet
on planes of dreams
and streams of thought
prayers
desires
yens
louder than closed mouths
and stubborn hearts
come together
as songs
or psalms
words to God
to heal the gap
...soul to speak
does that make us prayer warriors?
fighting the feelings?

I pray we get it right.

(I wrote this in my 44th year)

~444~

are there
four hundred
and forty-four
legions of angels?
are they here
for me?
will my forty-fourth year
be a foreboding
to the magic
that is the
best of my life
for the rest of my life?
fours in every corner
foundation
now, manifestation...
let the blessings,
come forth.

~policing~

as a people
born from stolen culture
to cultivate a land
we'd always be
policed…
it's no wonder
that policing
one another,
slaves enslaving slaves,
indoctrination
indelibly carved
whipped
lashed
into the blood
of the blood once shed…
our cells carrying
memories of imprisonment,
impressions
of their control
etched into our bones
so much so,
that we police ourselves
and our brethren
by second nature
…and yet to be aware,
we're free.

let your brothers and sisters
be free
free yourself

~pray away~

I'mma pray
you away...
rebuke you
into the heart
of another
let you hover
as they discover
your heart
can never be won
that they'll never be one
...not with you
the elusive
spiritual recluse
whose soul
seems sewn tight
with the might
of the darkest
starless night...
I'mma pray
you away...
refuse you
any parts
of a place
you evade
as if my touch
were made
of grenades
...I want you gone
pack your shit
every case you built
against me
why you're not suited for me...
and go.
I rescind
the love I sent
all the words
I kinda meant
just go!
stay away...I pray.

~so, who?~

they stood still
minds running haplessly,
feverishly scanning
over pages
already written and read,
fingering through memories
for moments to remember...
foreplay replayed...
ripples of sensory
and chemistry cascade
chills made
hands laid
waves...fade.
so, who touched you like me?

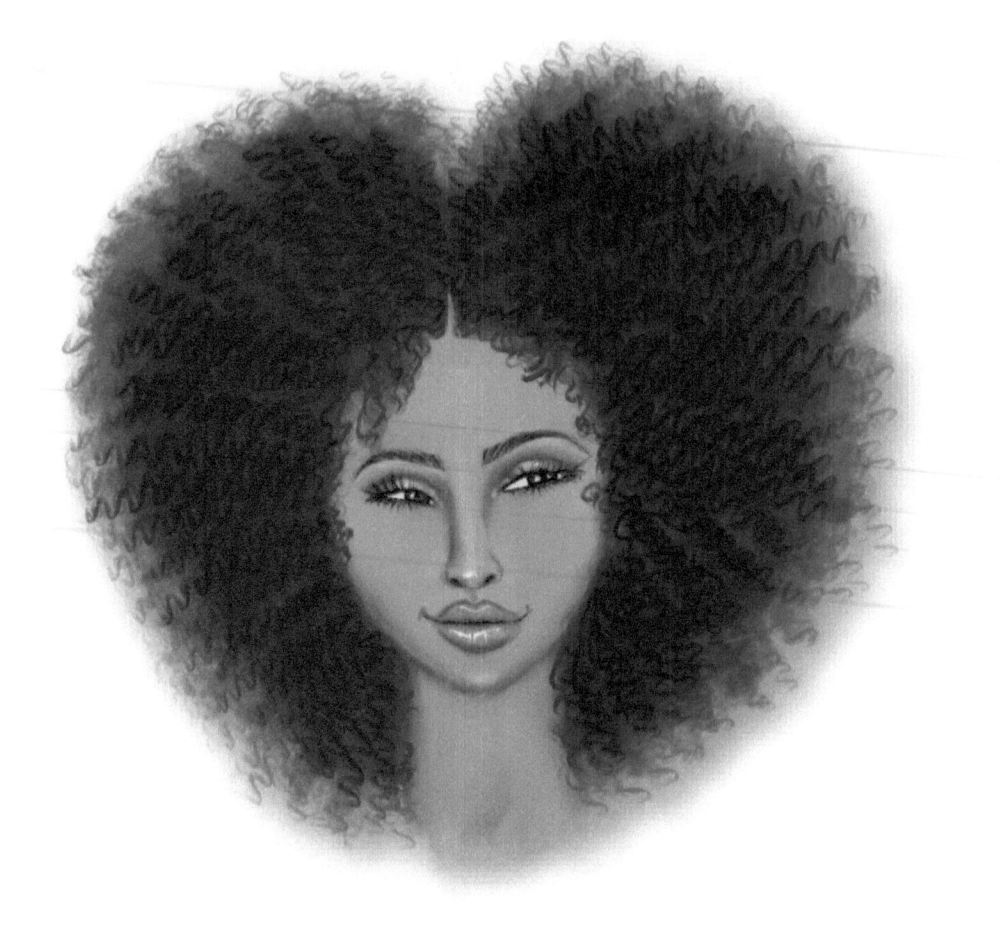

~for the best~

some soul mates
are trials in disguise
bringing with them
heartbreak and pain
this too,
is useful
because even a façade
can be truth…
how else can you
determine authenticity
but through falsity?
how else do you measure good,
except through
what's considered bad…
through the pretense of being a soul mate…
you can figure out who's *not*

~fear~

what most fear isn't love,
they fear rejection,
abandonment,
disappointment...
they fear
the ticking of time going by,
wasted on someone
not worth the wait...
they fear disloyalty,
betrayal,
perhaps even...
choosing wrongly

love is desired,
welcomed,
fantasized on
and romanticized...
love is impetus and impulsive
bubbling pots
and active volcanoes
so,
love isn't the fear of explosion,
it's the fear that
nothing will catch fire

most of us don't fear love...
we fear it won't kiss us,
dance with us,
woo our hearts and remain

we fear love's escape,
not it's hold

~astral angels~

there are times
I'm certain
that the angels
watching over me
are in collusion
with the angels
watching over you.
plotting perfectly timed dreams
with real time touch.
you're the only one
whose hands
touch me while I sleep,
as my earthly self fevers in response…
you're the only one
whose scent
is louder than delta waves
and whose eyes
penetrate astral darkness…
you come,
steal moments with me,
dipping in and out
of scenes concocted
from repressed consciousness
and then forget
where you've been
in the daylight…

I don't know
if the angels
that watch over me
scheme with the angels
that watch over you,
to keep us connected
beyond our will
shielding us from conscious recall…
but, I know *someone*
is asleep on the job
because I remember everything…

~true love~

the truest love
is founded on freedom
wings and breezes
life cast on the waters of
peace and release
no true love
was ever built upon
restraints
chains of insecurity
pretense of purity
or even the sense
of 100% certainty
the truest love
will keep its arms open
"agape"
for ease of embrace
and for ease of f r e e d o m...
the truest love allows
two to find
who they are
while getting lost
in one heart
the truest love
won't hurt you for long...
the pain of your tears
will jolt them out of their fears
and the arms of love
will either,
EMBRACE
or
LIBERATE...

love will not ignore
the void in need
it will not tap the source
until it is empty
living off of oblivion
thinking only of self
...*not* when it's true.

~ancestral memory~

when you tap into
the ancestral pulse of your origins,
revisiting the cradle...
tipping it slightly
allowing the creak of the wood
to help you remember
the folklore whispered
over closed lids
in the clearest,
starlit skies
of a country untouched
by the ravage
of greed and control...
you find your place
in the ancient tribes
of the motherland,
you turn off the white noise
from systematic programming
and clear your channel
for conscious awareness
of the macro-consciousness
from where you were seeded...
you hear the songs,
chants,
and drums
...and you can see yourself clearly
were you a fighter warrior?
a medicinal warrior?
village storyteller...
library to future generations?
did you dance a prayer?
were you a birth warrior...
ushering in life
to a growing tribe

when you tap into
the ancestral pulse of your origins...
what will you find?

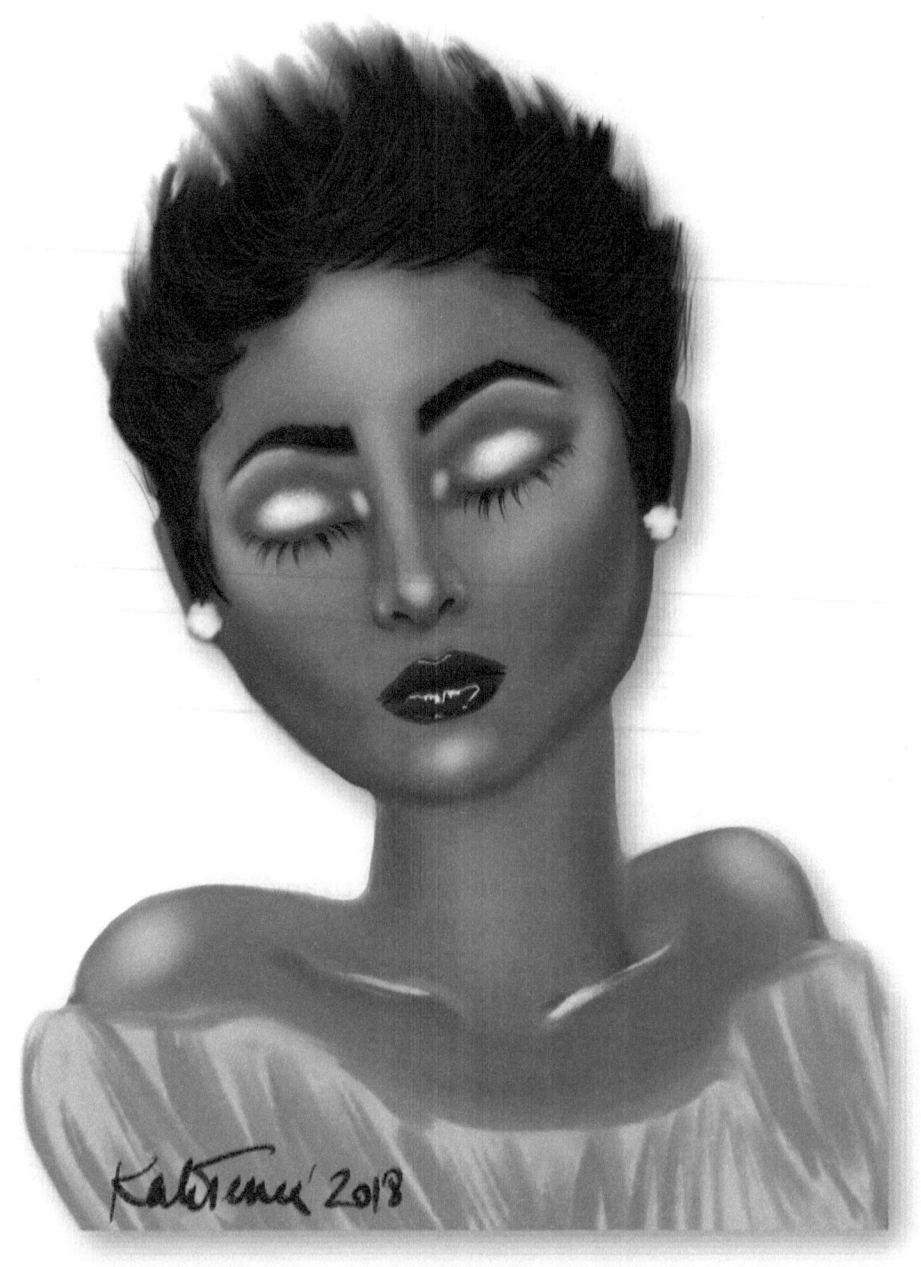

~letting go~

they left...
took the air with them
so that when you finally
breathed again
it was because
they passed you in a crowd...
the scent of before,
the scent of nostalgia,
the scent of residual love
traipsing about
plucking scenes from
your olfactory memory
plying you
to either stalk your past
or let go for posterity
because,
they left...
and with it
they took the air
the stale air
of brokenness
and abandonment
...the thick air of oppression
disguised as love
...so, letting go
is breathing again
fresh perspective,
floral notes of self-love,
the fragrance of new life
just. let. go.

when we fall in love, we find ourselves swirling in circles of passion, newness and fantastical manifestations of our most romantic daydreams. we see life in tandem with another, losing ourselves in the basking. that is, until we roll out of the bed of euphoria and into life's gauntlet. there, we're tasked with surviving the trials of daily life as it claws our loving vision with temptations and adversity. in those moments, we ask for grace...the ability to exhale and fall into the security that our love is safely nestled between each other's heartbeats. for that we are grateful, for that we become gracious...

~grace us~ [gracious]

bless the breath between us,
make it all the air we need...
make our kisses water for growth,
make us impervious to weeds...

bless the spaces we travel,
even the inches between our eyes...
make our words sweeter than
the salt and sand
we may track from the outside

thank you

~shame~

I prayed past
the shame...
attached to
my name and frame
that the stars
would gift me
a light in love
that would never
keep me cloaked
in the shadows
...shame on me
for buying
into the game
that my love belonged
in the darkness
of others' cowardice...
blame my brain
for thinking my heart
could love down
the walls of pain
disguised as
preconceived notions
of unworthy devotion
for a beauty
with a little more wave
in her ocean
damn the man
too weak to plan
a life with a queen
because she's not lean
I pray past
the time,
where I ain't
considered fine
all because
of the tight confines
of small minds...
for shame

~domestic violets~

her favorite color was blue…
cerulean,
sky's blue…
not the color of
burst veins or
purplish wounds,
not the color of
scarlet ire
or cowardice

she loved her blues
in bouquets of
irises and orchids,
not orchestrated monologues
of degradation,
not chords of
blackened force
or scenes of
muted blood…

she loved her violet drapes,
to close out the world,
not to hold
the graying darkness in…
not to hold in
the aches of brokenness
…she never wanted
anything more
than for her domestic violets
to be less violent
and more floral
less black,
more blue…
cerulean,
like the sky's blue

(for the survivors)

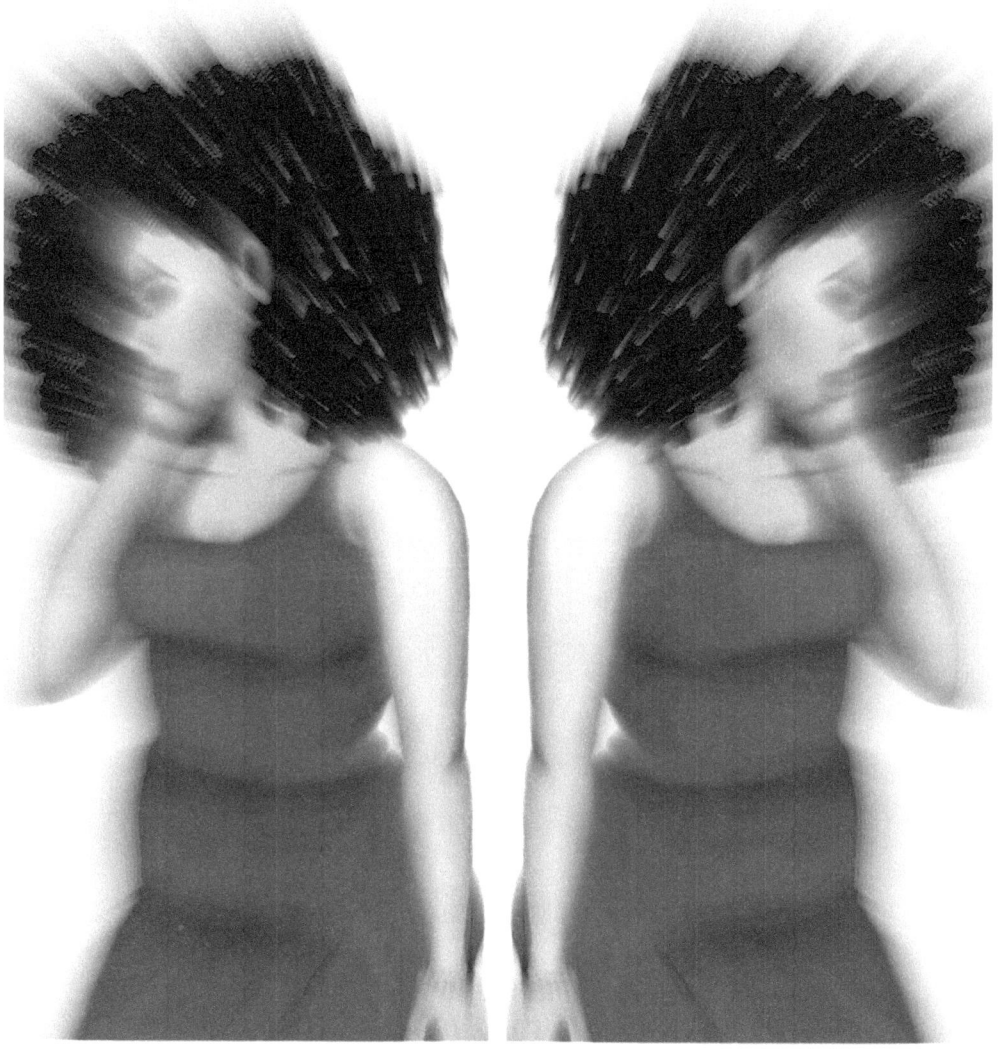

we hear so much about "old souls" being reborn into new bodies. we also know that some of those same people aren't even sure if they believe in reincarnation. (a lot of Christians and other believers of organized religion don't) so I reasoned that if we are indeed being reincarnated, then it makes sense that old souls get born into new life. if there is no such thing though, then what? how about the concept that souls are as ancient as the universe? stars or comets or the dust of planets post supernova are the living energy that governs humanity by way of birth. souls that hang suspended in time and light years, are awaiting portals to enter as new life. what if the oldest souls never lived a flesh bound life and were just the universe's "surplus" …awaiting a chance to be born?

~suspension~

amidst the galaxies
of burgeoning planets
and blinding suns,
floats souls older than age…
sparks of energy
awaiting to fall
from the blackness…
once stars,
now losing one kind of life,
to gain another,
to gain flesh…
ethereal recall
from billions of light years
guiding the soul,
to an open vessel
ushering them
into the human experience
this is where
the old becomes new
where ancient consciousness
enters into finite bindings
…what do you think?

~oddly enough~

I'm a moon in the daytime,
a sun in the night's sky...
a dove in the deepest sea,
a dolphin soaring in the air...
I'm the thing
you couldn't imagine,
and still the one
standing in front of you...
can you see me?
oddly enough,
I know you can't
oddly enough,
I don't want you to...
oddly enough,
you probably do
and don't want to...
what an odd pair we are

~blindsided~

I've walked into walls,
feeling the air for you…
asking angels
to show me your self
in a light I can recognize
with my eyes closed
…I've bruised myself,
nudging at you in the dark,
needing you to be
a torch on the way to love…
I get it now…
I've asked too much,
you sleep during the day
and I see best at night
we may never
touch again in this life
because,
we are both
blind to the other's side

~addict~

you could be
smoke dope
shoot up dope
capsule on your tongue
to the back
of your throat dope...
you could be
the connect
to the supplier
international ghost dope
and not be
what he wants
or even what you hope...
he's probably chasing
the high from
her thighs
addicted to
a dream
you can't see,
take it from me...
find *your* addict!

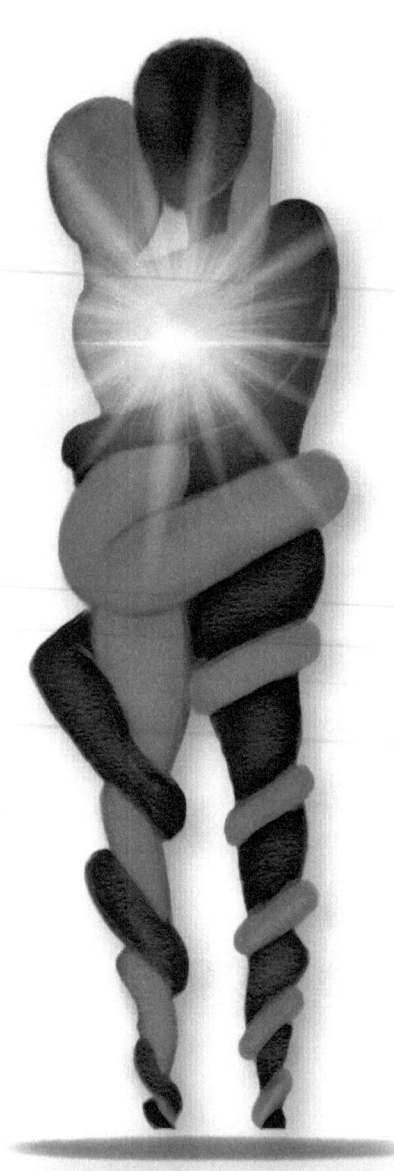

~smudges~

if love is coloring
outside the lines
friendship after love
is trying to
un-color the Picasso
how do you
paint by colors
an abstract passion?
how do you redo
strokes of genius
with broken crayons?
if love is smudging
the colors into one another
to blend,
friendship after love
is soaking the page
to blur the art.
you can't watercolor over oil...
you can't color over acrylic
love is smudges
on the fingertips
love is us on paper

so far we think we know what prayer is. we even think we know how to pray, but there's always the question as to "are we praying fervently?". do we mean what we aver? do we come with the most opened hearts, faithful that our spoken and thought words are echoing beyond the stars and into the ears of Whom we believe in? are we present in the presence of God? what are "we" doing?

~we~

we pray over light
burn oils for clarity
we honor colors
with symbolism
in stones of earth

we honor the unknown
with our most fervent devotions
not knowing
the honor is in us...
we hold space
for the presence of God,
but is He present in *us*?
how do *we* show up
within our own pleas
for mercy, chance, healing, discernment...?
prayer is part faith
and part works

we cannot become
so beholding to ritual
that we're not compliant
with our spiritual selves...
is not the word ritual *in* spiritual?

when do we show up
in the prayer
when do we
become prayer
by living a life of gratitude...
a breathing thank you
to the Creator
for the chance to do it again another day

I think that the reason we as a race of people struggle so much with being present in the now, is because we're no more linear than time. we're stuck, bound like feet in cement to the time on a clock that says this is now. live in the now…but, with intense memories of what was…even a lifetime ago. It's that same sense of memory that propels us forward past our current affairs into what will be. we're stars looking for a place to navigate to. it's innate and primal to want to connect it all like a wisp of oval light mapping out where we began with where we'll end. why else would we spend so much time trying to do the most before we 'die'?

~the long and short of it~

at times
our memories are
too long
our embraces
too short
we get stuck between
the pain of yesterday
and the yearning of today
we yen validation
through appreciation
to be soul seen
and flesh forgiven
healing is here
between the lines…
the nostalgia conjured,
the trauma we stir,
curdling like bad milk…
always sours the process
all we have to do
is decide…
to be whole
mended
and ready for
longer embraces
and shorter memories

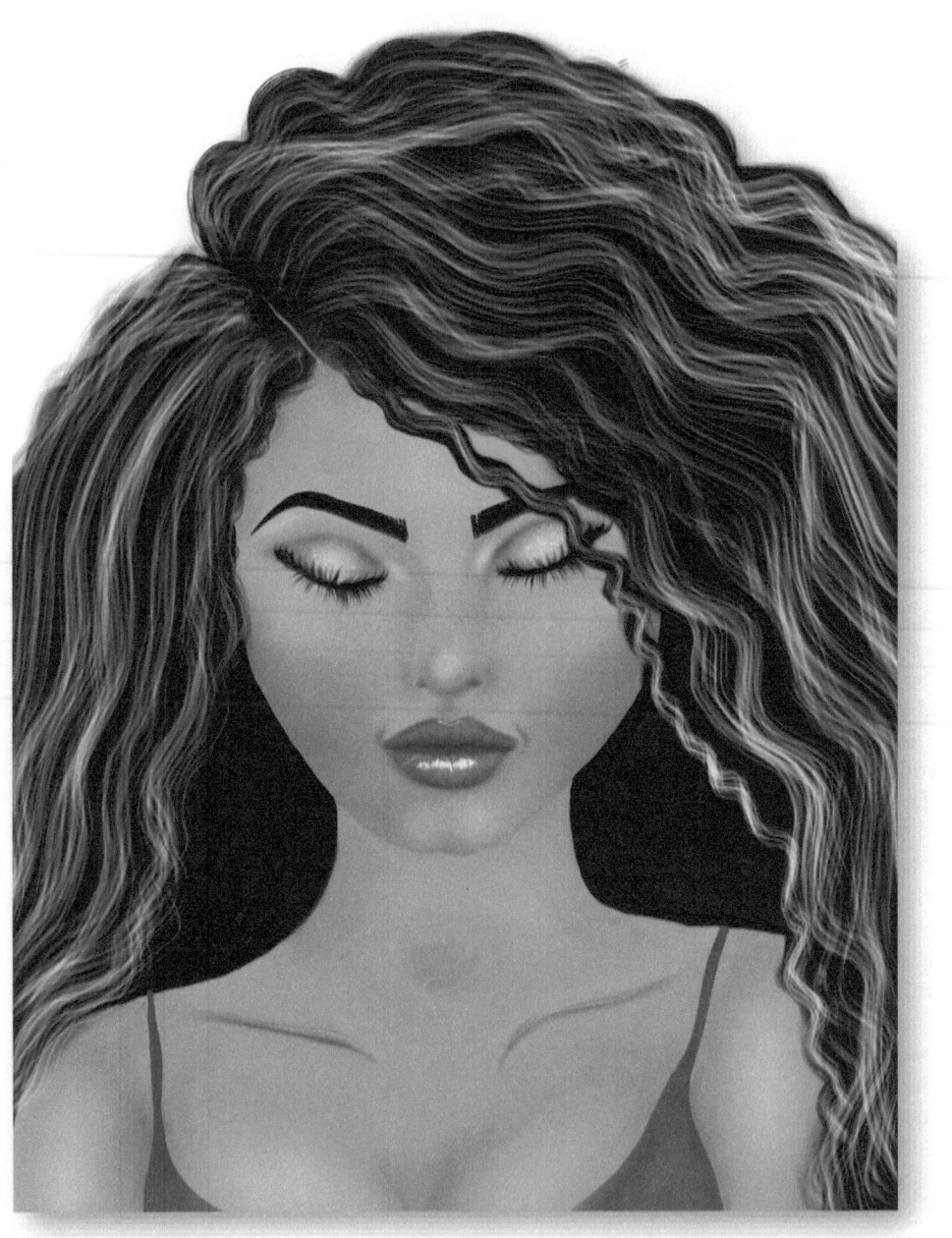

I'm learning to meditate wherever I am. no matter how frenetic the world around me becomes, I've learned to close my eyes and center myself. I will peace, envision a shield of light around me and I remind myself that I don't have to succumb to the noise. it's not always easy to find your Zen in the middle of mess, but it's possible. once you figure out who you are, what makes you happiest and fulfilled, you can tap into your happy place and emanate that outward to reinforce your immediate environment. yes, you can take your own energy and push it out against the vibrations threatening to encroach on your safe place.

~within and without~

though we clamor for oneness,
oneness starts with the one
connecting to self
then another
and so forth...
within,
we strengthen,
eye the past with
a magnifying glass
to focus on betterment
to heal the fractures bone deep
that keep us from sleep...
we find the places
where we tripped over pebbles
and walked into boulders
and built caution signs
for those ambling behind
and for ourselves,
traversing forward...
without this,
we become rudderless,
floating along
wheresoever the wind blows,
with whoever shows
no...we must go within
or we'll always be without,
without self-love,
awareness,
forgiveness,
understanding,
and peace...

we are in a season of manifestation...

everyone is learning to tap into their own god power from our God source, in order to attract to them the blessings they desire. we're seeing more people awaking and stepping into their self-awareness, understanding and doing away with antiquated boxed in ideologies that no longer serve them. all this is beautiful, well and good...but, what most aren't taking in consideration is the energy they entertain.

we are all living breathing molecules, atoms, etc. true science in the flesh...but spiritual and universal mysticism in the soul. we are a combination of being planted in the flesh and watered in the spirit.

there are certain plants that will not grow where others flourish. sunflower soil won't necessarily nurture roses. all things have to be considered. if you're trying to manifest a garden, but you have someone around you who is a weed...someone who oversaturates your ground with negativity or emotional weight...who pulls up your seedlings when you aren't looking...you will never see your blessings manifest. the environment simply doesn't allow for it. the energy you're trying to attract won't connect and spark the flame of endless blessings.

...if you aren't careful what energies are around you as you attempt to manifest, it will be like throwing seeds on cement. nothing will grow or show.

~tilling~

I found a spot
where the soil smelled of
richness and promise,
I took a seed
from my pocket of potential
and dropped it
into a hole I dug
with my bare hands...
I covered it gingerly
and used my tears for water
I left it under the sun for light
and when the moon hovered,
I watched the newest leaves
glisten with night dew...
when the flower bloomed,
seeing its success,
I repeated the process...
but as I was tilling,
I got caught up
in the busyness
of green thumbing,
I hadn't noticed
something was eating
my garden's bounty...
I stopped to tend to
the ravaged flower
only to find my seeds
were being dug up
the newer flower's buds,
pulled by the root...
it took me a bit
to realize that
the one damaging my garden
was someone I let in...
my garden now has barbed wire.

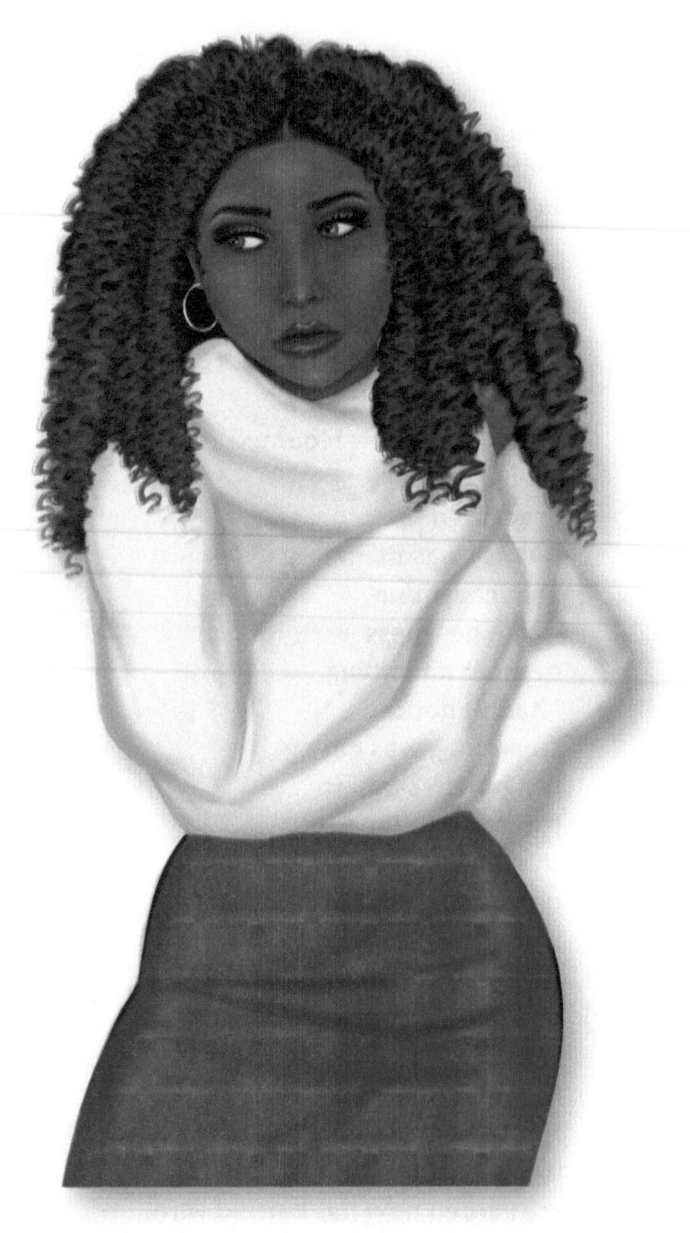

I've written so many poems about angels and time. I've been fastened to the concept of how we connect as humans to something otherworldly. we imagine that beyond our own stratosphere into space is where God dwells. I've spent many a midnight hour, searching for God behind planets, in wormholes and within the star-dusted designs of nebulae and galaxies...

one day, it hit me as I watched a movie about Stephen Hawking. I am not saying this is 100% the case, but what if the space beyond our planet and the galaxies beyond our galaxy and the universes beyond our universe...in their endless light years away...aren't where God can be found. what if all that black, peppered with sparkles and beams of light are His mind. What if we're INSIDE of a consciousness and therefore the reason we'll never lay eyes on the face of God.

~God thought~

perhaps,
why we may never "see"
the face of God
is because
we're at a skewed vantage point...
what if
we are a part of
a god consciousness,
a created thought
within a created realm
in the mind of
a supreme being
with a view
of a universe beyond ours...
what if
we're sparks of light
within an unending flame?
what if
we're on the inside
looking out,
but never past...
just a god thought.

that would mean we're created in a realm that lives in a cell in the brain of an entity far bigger than us. we're thoughts, fashioned realities within a dream, the result of a thought process.

...and if we happen to be made in His image...then that means we too have the power to create realities, galaxies, planets...life. can you imagine if all the dreams you've had are actual parallel places, with existing timelines and circumstances? does that mean the earth I dream of where there are three suns and two moons is a real place?

Imagine the power...now imagine that power is backing you with the guidance of angels created to keep you aligned with everything meant for your highest good.

~back up drive~

I got back up...
I know with every step
there's a coordinating step
I can't see but feel
there's a hand to my back,
a gentle push in the right direction,
a comforting hand of consolation...
I get back up,
because there's a driving force,
helping me navigate life
each misstep a recalculation
of how to get
where I'm supposed to be
even when I worry,
I'm not worried...
I got back up

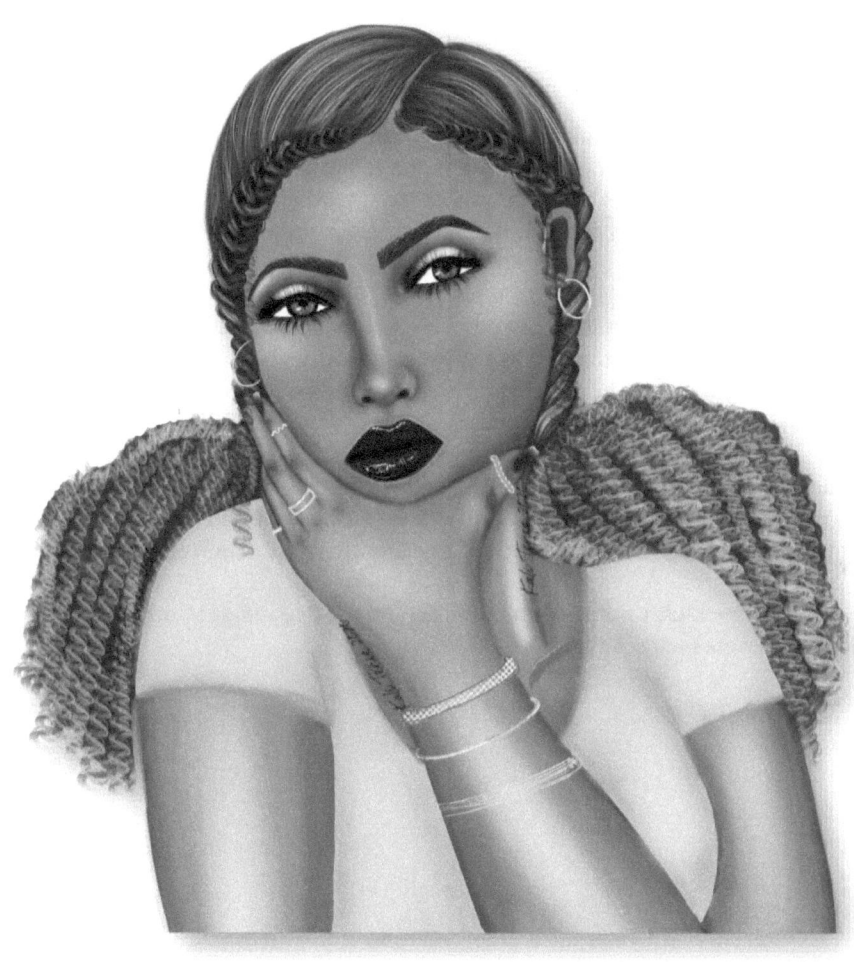

In closing...

whether we're speaking of love with a mate, love of family and friends or love of self...most of us endeavor to find that love within our lives. most of us are trying to find the divine purpose in our careers and desires. we're looking to align our deepest wants with our highest sense of purposefulness.

society puts upon us the weights of success, accomplishment, validation and appropriate behaviors, but they're veiled (not so thinly) in the constructs of tiered and numbered goals. we don't always find our gifts and purposes especially, when we're bogged down with the constant reminders fed to us to reach the finish line. for some that's school, others it's work, for the rest it's family...

yet, there is more to life than that. our passions and talents are as important as any bottom dollar. we're *more* than 40-hour weeks and holiday bonuses. we're community work, artistic expression, literature begat from pain and love...love drenched in sweet sighs of fulfilled bliss, political movements with raised fists and silent tears...

we're connected threads in quilted oneness and we deserve to feel the beauty and peace that comes with knowing ourselves, to know others...so MAY be we can touch the love God feels for us...to quite possibly know the touch of angels watching and universal synchronicity.

...to experience the bluish-purple light of Indigo and see beyond our frames and finite realities. to become Indigo Angels.

Thank you.

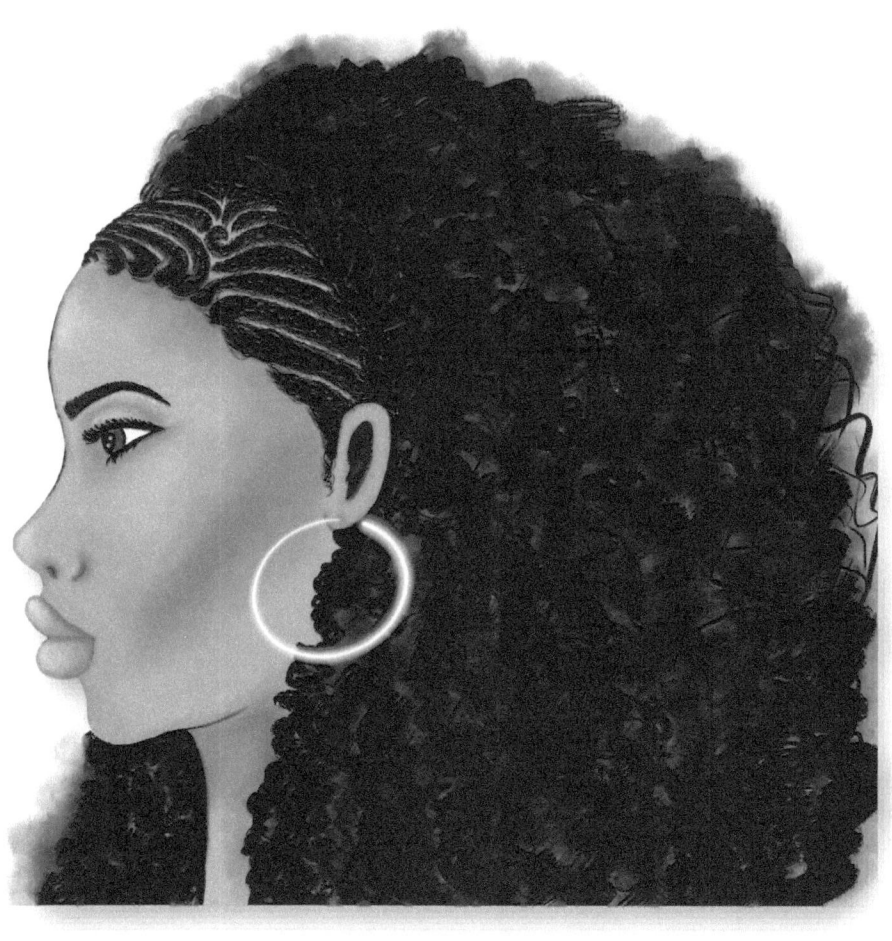

www.ingramcontent.com/pod-product-compliance
Lightning Source LLC
Chambersburg PA
CBHW020617220526
45463CB00006B/2605